Dear Andre,

 May your world be
filled with the surprise
of Love, and happiness!
You have an incredible
future coming~

♡ Deirdre

Will

Love and Light!

Endine Baloglu

# THE (not so) LITTLE BOOK OF SURPRISES

WORDS FROM THE MYSTICAL VISION AND POETRY
OF DEIRDRE HADE

PHOTOGRAPHS AND IMAGES
BY ENDRE BALOGH

CREATED BY WILLIAM ARNTZ

## FOREWORD

Why a Book of Surprises? Can a surprise be expected? What is a surprise anyway? Webster's defines a surprise as "an attack without warning."

**WAIT A MINUTE**. This is not a high school English paper. It is, rather... well, we're not going to tell you. It won't be a surprise if we do.

Surprises run the gamut from life-threatening earthquakes to ecstatic gifts. From the phone call informing of a tragic car wreck to your favorite comedian's rip-roaring punch line. Although varied in the extreme, all these have something, or things, in common. The "you" before is different from the "you" afterwards, and that difference is profound.

**YOUR BODY LITERALLY CHANGES.** The chemical makeup of your emotional hormones, or peptides, has completely shifted. An eighty-year-old grandmother can suddenly pick up the car that has fallen on her favorite grandchild. Your psychological state changes. The depression you've been living in for twenty years evaporates in an instant when those lottery numbers match up. Even your perception of physical reality changes. Suddenly, everything is brighter after that very first kiss from your heartthrob.

And just so we don't surprise you too much, we're gonna let the cat out of the bag, at least a little bit, and let you know why a collection of **DEIRDRE HADE'S** spiritual insights and **ENDRE BALOGH'S** photographs and images, have coalesced into a book of surprises.

## THE "YOU" BEFORE IS DIFFERENT FROM THE "YOU" AFTERWARDS.

Transformation is the name of the game in spiritual practice. Meditation, mindfulness, prayer, vision quests, seeing The Master—all the techniques of the path are about changing who you are.

Of course, not all surprises take the "surprisee" to a more aware, enlightened state. While finding a frog in your knapsack may produce a sweet chuckle, finding a cobra will not. Although both will change you, it's best to have the person monkeying with your destiny lines be someone who is wise.

**SOME SURPRISES ARE TIME BOMBS.** In my time with Spiritual Teachers I have often heard them say something that seemed ridiculous, only to witness what they said played out in front of my astonished eyes some months later. In this sense, you could say that simply revealing the hidden is always a surprise.

**AND, MY OH MY, ARE THE SAGES, MYSTICS AND ORACLES GOOD AT THAT.**

Life can get boring. What's that? Do you hear that buzzing? No wait—is it music? Is it building!? Oh My—let's dance.

– William Arntz

ONE POUND

HONEY

## In The Honey Jars

Am I really alive
        Am I really here?

I wandered on the stardust
        to understand the question
    to try to know what
        recollections made had left me here
unknown and unseen.

A mysterious hand pushed me on
        until I asked who and what it is, "I Am."

A creation of primordial thought?
        I scurried about on the edge of doubt.
    I lived outside time within the shadow place
        until I met the naked emptiness,

the nothingness of me—

and the solutions I thought I had
        were only empty jars of honey

laughing on a sun-filled window shelf,
        a chorus of honey jar ghosts
            crying more, more, more,
Honey.

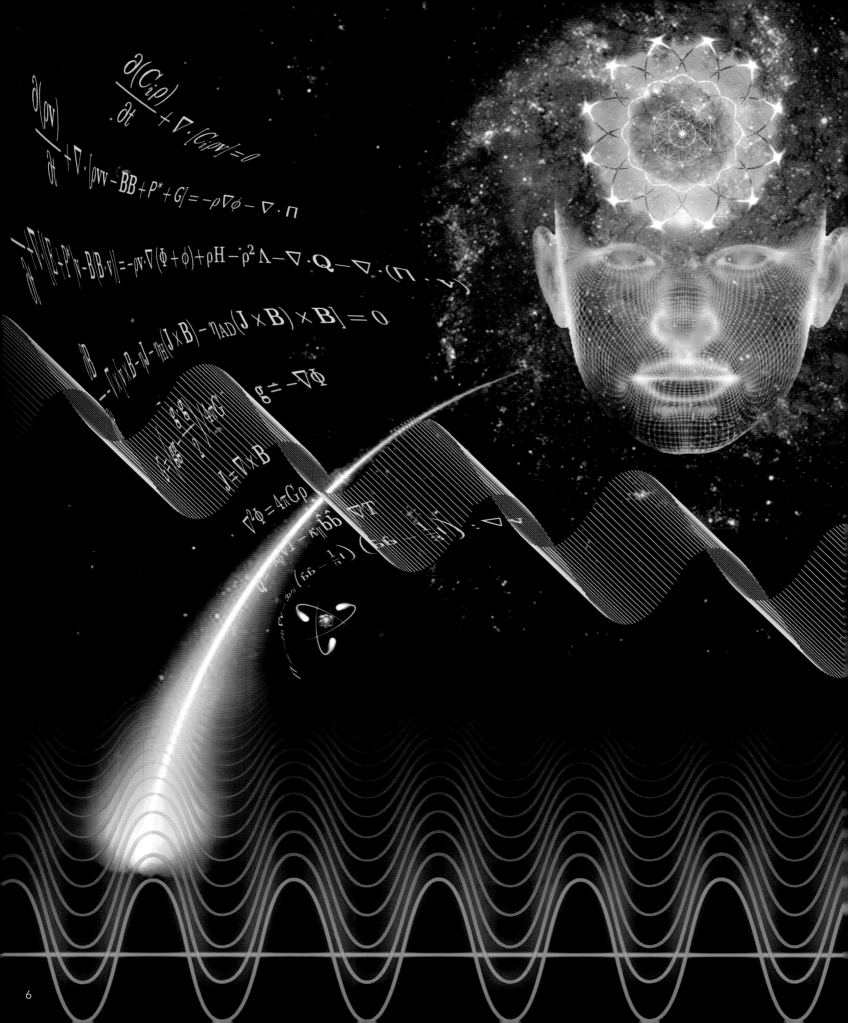

WE ARE HERE AT A TIME
OF NEW BEGINNINGS.
IT IS A TIME TO RETHINK
EVERYTHING THAT YOU
HAVE LEARNED.

IT IS A TIME TO TAKE
PERCEPTION AND TURN
IT ON ITS HEAD.

We are here as m
here you are a m
born a mystic an
mystic.

And there's
no way you're
going to get
out of it.

ystics. If you are

ystic... You were

d you will die a

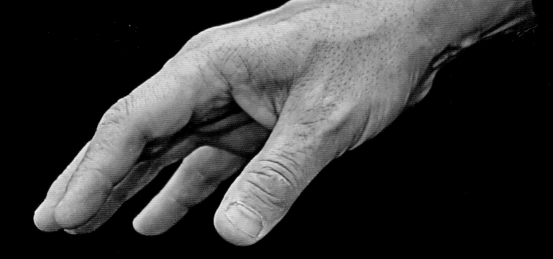

The heavens above are torn. The fabric of creation has a rent.
The divisiveness of the human mind, the split, is causing one side
of the curtain to go one way and the other to go another way.
The tear is ascending to the throne of God.

Quickly we come to sew it up. If the tear makes it all the way to
the Godhead, our reality will cease to exist. It will dematerialize
and return into nothingness.

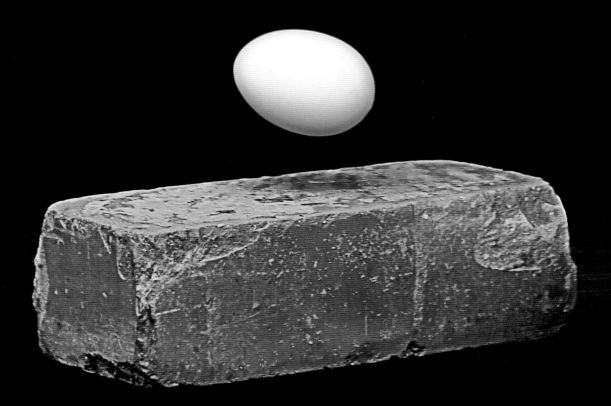

*Every point of light, every star is an aperture into the throne of God, the pure realms of heaven. Each opening, each aperture, is a "Shining One" holding the gates of reality open so you remember where you came from and what you are here to do, and these apertures of light you call stars.*

*Now switch your perception of the third dimension. See the stars not as round spheres but as open doorways. Now press your awareness through the myriad of stars, the constellation you know as your astrology, astronomy. Press your being through these holes, these openings, then take a deep breath and enter into the world of pure light.*

*Now experience yourself in both worlds and **just play**.*

You are at a choice point—**a choice point.** One of

the rare times in the incarnation of the human where

you **choose what the next million years**

**are going to look like,** and your generation,

and the generations of the next twenty years. You are the

generation that has been given the **duty to choose.**

It is time to step into the shoes of that which created you and that which sent you forth into this world. *It is time to gather.* It is *time to find one another.* It is *time to heal*, for the seed that was placed within us, the seed of forgetfulness, was placed so that we would learn new patterns, a new path home.

If the patterns had been laid we would not be the explorers, the discoverers, the warrior hunter/ huntress. If the light had been shown, the great phoenix would have no purpose, nothing to rise from. If the mystery had not been placed, we would not become a creator. *For you are here to be a creator, a creator of your life.*

TRUE THOUGHT AND PRESENCE IS WITHIN
THE SILENCE. IT IS WITHIN THE PAUSE
BETWEEN THE SYLLABLES AND THE PAUSE
BETWEEN THE BREATH.

THIS PAUSE IS INFINITY.
THIS PAUSE IS WHERE
WE GO TO EMBODY THE
MYSTERY OF FULLNESS.

The outer world is a holographic picture of your mind.

You are separate from every other mind, while you are a unique ray of light.

This is the paradox—while you are separate from every other mind, you are at the same time "one" with every other mind, every other thing in the universe.

There is no other light like your ray.

Your ray is so important and so needed on the planet right now.

It is not possible to have a ray that is not needed.

**While,**
at the same time that
**you** are separate and
**you** are different and
**you** are unique,
**you** are **one** and the
same with all of **creation.**

*We are the conduit for harmony and yet all we create is chaos.*
*Harmony must come from within. When opposing energies inside of*
*you are married in union, **you have internal peace.***

*When this union happens **you wake up.** You realize that you are the*
*center of the universe. You are the axis mundi. You are the heart, the*
*body of "All That Is."  Then you **fall in love with life.** You run, you*
*create, you paint a painting, you build a ship, you do all of this—and*
*the Creator, in order to be whole, **pours himself into your heart.***
*And without us doing this, the Creator is forever separate.*

*The three highest* emanations of the *Tree of Life*—truth, wisdom, and understanding, equal all of the aspects of love, union and forgiveness. And we are here as human beings to be the **conduit** between the **elements of creation.**

There was a time when you knew how to understand nature's language. Listen and she will teach you of stars and realms of magical things, of truth and wisdom unseen. For when you learn to speak to her again, all of nature will be your friend.

There's a map where you can choose to go to God. You don't have to wait for, "Oh my God, it's happened! Ahhk! It's gone. How do I get it back?"

God actually wrote a map, a code, so that you could enter into God's joy, happiness, and bliss whenever you want to.

My question to you is, how many illuminations have you had that you didn't take in and were wasted? Just think about that for a minute. Do you think there were illuminations, true prophetic experiences for you, that came and you did not open to them? You walked right by. Well, the answer is yes, you've had a few.

# That Mystical World

that's where we find the Light,

but it's also the chrysalis

of coming undone.

If you're going to embark on

a journey of coming undone,

you damn well better

have your ducks in a row,

because it could be like

"splat" on the windshield.

# The Silent Watcher

is a place, an all-seeing eye, of just watching and observing yourself in everything you do. The more that this eye opens, the more you begin to see into your inner being, the more you will understand who you are, what makes you tick and what brings you joy and sorrow. From the Silent Watcher, you begin to see a world you've never seen before. You begin to see who you really are, without all of the brainwashing you've received throughout your life.

*The experiences of the human existence are like*
*weights on a ship.* **The negativities are anchors.**
*What we call the negativities that bring us grief*
*and suffering—in our selves,*

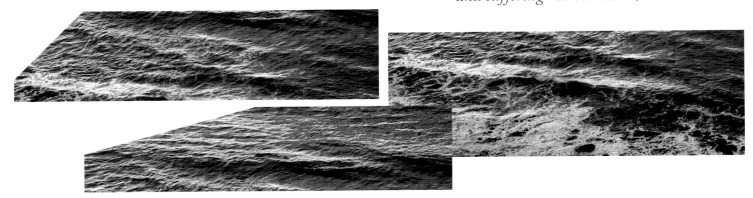

*our family, our country, our world. These*
*negativities are light, but they are the broken light.*
*They are the stars that have become black holes.*

*This world is tough.*
*It's a tough place for a spirit to be.*

*This is not an easy land. It's hard. If you fall*
*and hit a rock, you break your head open.*
*I mean, what's that about? It's not like*
*that anywhere else.*

*In the human experience there is a great*

*imbalance in the negativities of broken light.*

*This has damaged our nervous system, damaged*

*our electrical light system, damaged the perfection*

*of the DNA structure that we call "the human*

*body" and all of the levels of consciousness in*

*our subtle bodies.*

*We are seeing this now in epic proportions,*

*negative energy that turns into evil. Tragically,*

*these negative energies are what we use to*

*anchor our spirit into the third dimension.*

*It is time to anchor ourselves in another way.*

*It is time to pray.*

*Prayer is your most powerful anchor.*

In our world, the **systems are all fragile.**

Everything is, so we now have the extreme

control factor coming out of the woodwork,

because in the consciousness of our whole self,

that part of our self is now going, **"Control,**

**control, control. Squeeze in, squeeze**

**in, squeeze in.** Let's go back to 1900,

the good old days." Right? "When we had

control." That's what we're seeing, isn't it?

All around the world.

It is the collective consciousness of that fear,

the ego construct of that fear, attempting to

solidify something that cannot be solidified.

**Because it is false.**

The old paradigms are falling apart and people are grappling to try to find a way to pull them together. Somebody has to be the glue to hold the space for the love of the beings of Light—the Pistis Sophia, the Archangels of Light, the Ascended Masters—to come and help us redeem our world.

Because we cannot do this alone.

We cannot.

Our Creator, the Archangels and Ascended Masters
are praying that you begin to see beyond the veils of
this world, because when you can truly see, you will
receive the access code, your key to enter into the
alternative reality of Oneness.

When you **enter into the Now** that is beyond the time-space creation, the new time will be created, and this new time does not have decay and disease. When you understand this, the Now, the point of presence, will create the new time.

## Time and space will not look the same.

This will happen over many, many lifetimes, because if it were to happen in this moment, the ego structure, the structure of the mind of the human, **would go mad and lose its mind.**

There is an entire **new wave of deeply conscious souls birthing,** and it's our job to create a new world for them; otherwise, they're going to hit the assault of our unconscious world—and a lot of them we're going to lose. They're going to be sacrificed, because they are of a different frequency. When they experience the lies of our world, they will fracture.

## These souls are coming as service.

We need them. Our planet needs them. If they do not make it, the old way of existing will destroy our world, of which **these souls are a part.**

**The Gates of your Reality are opening.**

*You are entering into the age of the mystical, the rebirth of mystery. Here, you will begin a sojourn home. Thus, I who have travelled with you, protecting you, caring for you, guiding you, lest the seed of your magnificence be lost. I have a path to bring you home, a path to return you to your brilliance.*

*For I am but a particle of myself in this physical world. My true self lives in the grand mansions of Light, our home, where you once walked beside me as one of the great Shining Ones—Star Beings, Angels of Light, Radiant Ones—shining through the galaxy. My light of hope is upon you as you journey in search of a way back home.*

*For you are my children. And I am Patience.*

# In The Honey Jars

The slippery belt of Orion's loop cast my spirit
into the Milky Way
where I lay
dormant for 2000 years
to contemplate
the beginning and the end,

silently watching over the jars of honey.

Then, on one millennium day
I spotted a few bees
around the node of Andromeda,

"Why are you here?" I asked,
"So far away from home?"

humm— buzzz— humm—

the honey bees replied:

"Delicate is mother who gives honey from her hive,
while your spinning galaxy searches to survive."

I made the decision to take this all into consideration.

On my personal journey of awakening I met many obstacles and many hindrances. I met many doubts.

I came to learn that all of these were the flames which would temper and hone my soul into a Sword of Light. With this sword, I can face any obstacle.

I discovered that I may not be able to get my brain to be the super brain that it will be ten or twenty thousand years from now, but I realized that by attaching myself to the **Light of Wisdom** every morning I could live in the creative synchronicity of God.

*By allowing yourself to expand your consciousness through your thinking, by changing your behavior for the better through action, your DNA will go through a metamorphosis. Your DNA will change and rearrange its structure. This is at the core of all healing. As you do this, you are actually assisting evolution to move along.*

Evolution and creation are the same thing. This is what it means to be in co-creation.

You have thoughts that you don't know about; it's called your unconscious mind. You have thoughts that you don't know about; it's called the neighbors. I'm not kidding. You have thoughts that you don't know about and it's called coming through the TV, coming through the iPad, coming through the phone. They're coming all the time through the airwaves.

You are bombarded with thoughts, which is why the processor, your brain, is going a little haywire. Not a little, but a lot haywire. Your immune system is tanking because the master gland, your brain, is in the middle of all this chaos. It's hitting you where your imagination is centered, where your thoughts all begin. That part of your brain that creates your reality is completely overloaded and stressed out. How can you create a new reality in this environment?

Then, we feel: *"Things are a little odd. What's going on here?"* But no one can name it, because we're in it. It's like we're in a fishbowl and the water is slowly turning colors.

*"Gee, do you think the water is a little bluer than it used to be?"*

*"I don't know."*

*"No, it's the same to me."*

*"Oh, I don't know..."*

*The brain is malfunctioning because the world is malfunctioning, and the world is malfunctioning because the brain is malfunctioning.*

*And if you want to see a malfunctioning brain go to Times Square.*

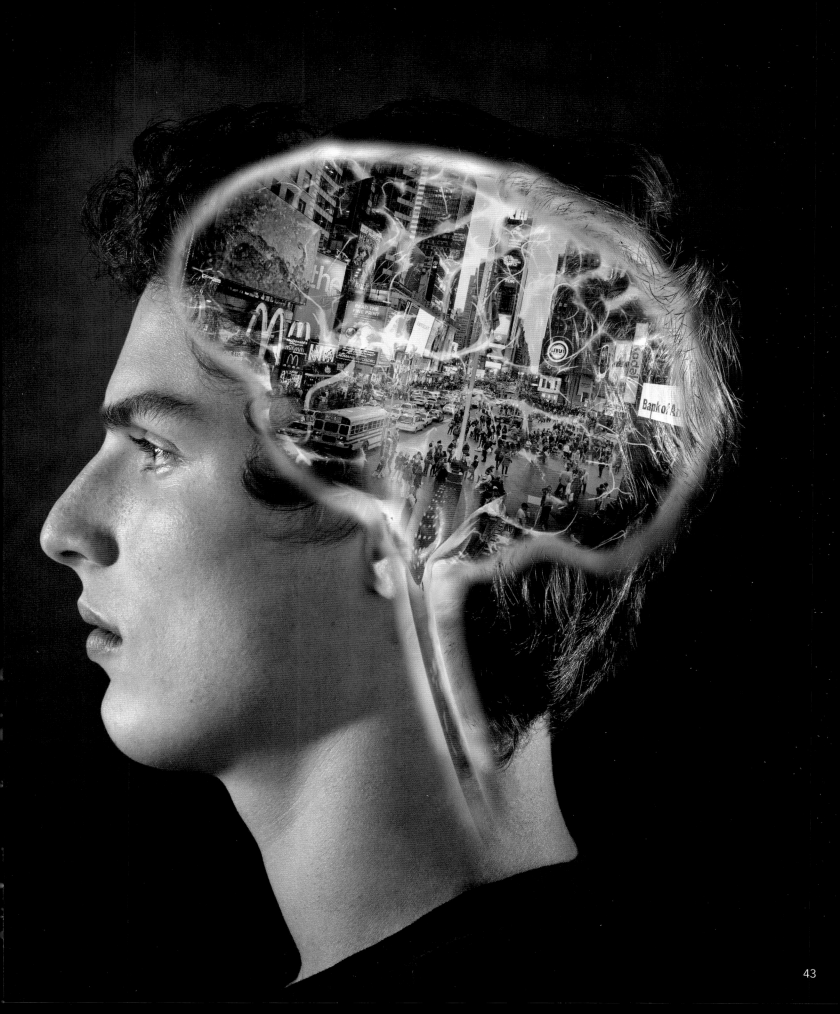

The operating system that we are living in is not efficient. It doesn't conserve energy. It's not putting us on the joy ride. We're not on the freedom train. It is each of our jobs, as individuals, to journey within, to learn, to know, and then to repair our operating system. To be able to say, "I am a creator and I choose to repair a system that I was given but that cannot sustain who I REALLY am."

And, what if you're someone who's coming in to bring the new words of the great Light Beings—the new words built on the old words, built on the ancient texts?

But those ancient texts, do they translate in your life when you're at the grocery store and somebody bumps you and yells at you? Do those ancient texts support you when you're driving down the highway and get flipped off? Do they support you, can they truly feed you, in the fast-paced world of the 21st century? Where's the map? How do we read the old texts in a new way?

We're from the future, *but our bodies, our brains, our minds, are not fully developed yet. So the body has limitations. It dies. It breaks. It regenerates itself if you cut your finger, why doesn't it regenerate an arm if you lose an arm? When you look at it at the molecular level, you should be able to grow an arm. They can grow seeds of arms in petri dishes. Why can't we grow an arm?* It's because the "who we are" is not here yet in the physical matter.

God *doesn't just pour the light in, because* *we're not ready.* The light is powerful. *The light purifies any darkness, and just like if* *you stand in the shower and you* open your mouth *to that beautiful water, if all of a* *sudden the Amazon River poured on you, you'd* *be dead.* You're not strong enough yet to withstand that amount.

This world of pain and suffering and life and
death and all of the confusions, this is not the
world of your soul, and so the soul is afraid:
*"Where am I?" "What is this place I got
dropped into?"*

The soul's reality is in the light—no disease,
no confusion, no war, no body that's breaking.
It's scary when the body starts to break.
I get a cut: *"Oh my God, I have a cut."*

The soul doesn't understand.

You must become the shepherd of your soul, care for your soul, talk to your soul. *"I know it's really scary out there soul, I got you covered, okay? I put on my mittens, I have a coat. You won't freeze to death."* Talk to your soul, because the soul is young here. In the worlds of light the soul is infinitely wise. Got it all together. Wings. *"Yo, I can fly."* The soul comes here, it's like, *"Oh, where did my superpowers go? My wings? Ahhhhhck."*

The soul doesn't know what to do.

*Remember, your body*
*is the Universe. "All That Is"*
*is inside. The two sides of your body, left*
*and right, as they are in balance, and your*
*heart-brain-heart-brain, as they are in balance, as*
*your inner world and outer world become balanced—*
*when these six directions are connected with attention,*
*you will enter into knowledge, the Kingdom Within,*
*the Other Side. This is a miraculous place to be.*
*It doesn't mean you don't have bad days, but*
*the bad days are not going to be*
*like they used to be.*

# The Little Princess

I was flying through the universe late one summer night. There, I came upon another reality. Floating among the stars was a giant seedpod, like a cocoon. I flew closer to find that it was not a seedpod at all, but a shimmering bronze lamp, like Aladdin's lamp. Just then a voice from inside the lamp cried, *"Let me out! Let me out!"*

My curiosity wanted, needed to know whose lamp-sealed voice this was. I must inquire, go inside, find out, fly into the belly of the lamp, squeeze through its long curved spout. Inside, a gigantic oval of white cotton light. In the distance a young girl with long black hair was jumping up and down waving at me. She wore brightly colored pantaloons, an embroidered top, on her head a jeweled headband. From it a transparent veil flowed. Her voice intrigued me, a voice not understood until my eyes reached her small form. For in an instant i was right in front of her. A brilliant blue sapphire sat in the middle of her forehead.

*"Who are you?"* She asked fiercely.

*"Who are you?"* I retorted.

*"I am a princess. My father locked me up inside of this lamp thousands of years ago. I am so mad at him. I have work to do and I have to grow up and get out of this lamp if I am going to do it."*

JUST THEN GOD SPOKE. A THOUSAND TINY MICROPHONES PRESSED INTO THE LAMP'S SHELL. THE LITTLE PRINCESS AND I BECAME VERY STILL NOT WANTING TO MISS GOD'S VOICE.

GOD SPOKE FIRST TO THE LITTLE PRINCESS. IN A STERN VOICE, "I AM GOD YOUR FATHER AND I LOCKED YOU UP FOR A REASON. IT WASN'T TIME FOR YOU TO BE FREE YET. YOU WOULDN'T HAVE BEEN SAFE."

GOD THEN SPOKE TO ME. "THIS IS MY DAUGHTER AND THIS IS YOU. YOU ARE THE LITTLE PRINCESS, AND YOU ARE THE ONE WHO MUST FREE HER. DO THIS AND YOU WILL KNOW MANY THINGS."

THE LITTLE PRINCESS THEN LOOKED UP AT ME WITH DARK LUMINOUS EYES, *Thank you for coming to find me.*

GOD CONTINUED, "YOU SEE, YOU MUST HAVE A QUEST. IF I BROUGHT YOU ALL KNOWLEDGE YOU WOULD NOT BECOME WHAT YOU WERE MEANT TO BECOME. YOUR SEARCH FOR TRUTH, YOUR THIRST FOR WISDOM, YOUR TENACITY AND PERSISTENCE TO FIND YOURSELF, THIS IS WHAT SHOWS ME IF YOU ARE READY TO RECEIVE MY KNOWLEDGE. YOU MUST DISCOVER, LEARN ON YOUR OWN. THIS IS HOW I CREATED YOU. NOW TAKE MY DAUGHTER WITH YOU. PROTECT HER, CARE FOR HER AND ILLUMINATION IS YOURS."

I PICKED UP THE LITTLE PRINCESS, CRADLING HER IN MY ARMS. WE DISSOLVED INTO A FRAGRANCE OF ROSE, SANDALWOOD, AND JASMINE. THE LAMP DISAPPEARED. I WOKE UP TO THE MORNING SUN FILLING MY ROOM SAFFRON GOLD, OUTSIDE A MEADOWLARK SINGING.

**This world is an illusion.**

*Your ego says it's real but you
know this place is an illusion.*

*So play with it.
Bend it. Mold it.
It's Jello, it's Silly Putty.*

*You will be happy the day you
realize you are dreaming this
whole thing up—the illusion.*

*However, **respect your illusion**.*

*I mean concrete is concrete.*

*One day you'll say,*

*"I'm in another world." It will*

*happen. You'll have glimpses where*

*you are literally in another world—*

***more real than this world**. And*

*when that happens, you will have*

*entered in. That will really mess*

*with your head. **Those worlds are***

***more real than this one.***

# HOW DO YOU KNOW IF IT'S GOD'S VOICE OR NOT?

This is an important question for freedom. You learn the voice of God by developing the skill and the mindfulness to be able to think deeply and broadly on an issue. There is an art to thinking well. Most people do not think well; therefore, they make decisions that aren't well, and then, there you go.

When you know how to think deeply and broadly, you become attuned to the very subtle frequencies of God, and in that way you detect the differences in frequencies between the false God and the real God. You won't know they're different until you are able to read that energy, until you have that sensibility, because the false God—is kind of like a knockoff. If you have a designer bag and see one for sale on the corner, you know it's a knockoff, but most people won't know.

So it's like that.

# THE FALSE GOD'S A KNOCK OFF.

# FEAR IS A CONSTRUCT

*Fear is a construct. That is all.*

Fear is a construct in the architecture of your mind. Fear causes your thoughts to become incongruent, out of balance. Just like a building, when you are out of integrity, out of alignment, the brick and mortar of your mind weakens. There is no stability. You become susceptible to negative influences. You crumble.

That energy field that we're all running, living in, is so weak that it had to devise ways to trick us into believing that it was really powerful, but it is not.

*Fear's greatest fear is that it will fall.*

# Integrity of Form is Virtue.

*Build a new house, a house of virtue.*

Virtue has integrity the same way a well constructed house has integrity. When you practice virtue, you build a strong mind. When you have a strong mind, your energy field becomes sacred geometry, a pyramid, a cube, an octagon, a geodesic dome. You experience inner stability. You live in peace.

Virtue is a power field whose energy has yet to be tapped. Tap the well of virtue and fear will disappear, truth will overcome darkness. The architecture of order and harmony is vastly stronger than that of lies.

Virtue. Faith. Truth. Love. Build these into the structure of your everyday life, and you will be free, you will know serenity.

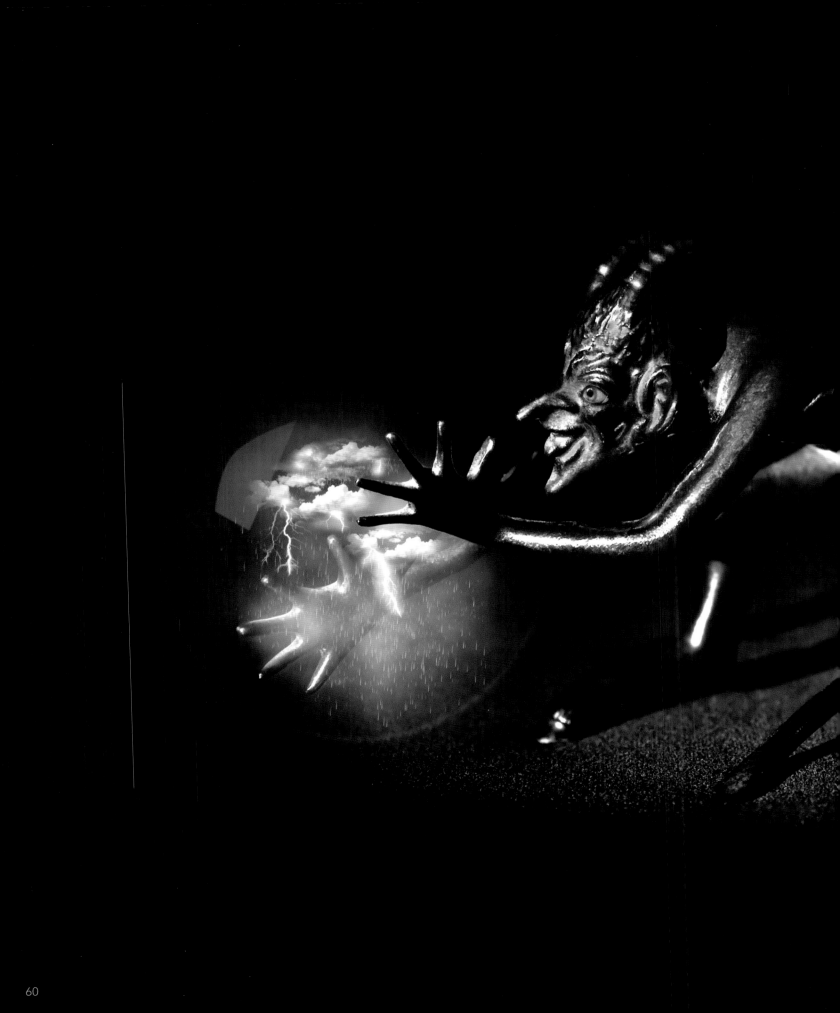

YOU HAVE ALLOWED THE LIGHT TO BE THE MASTER BECAUSE YOU DON'T KNOW WHO YOU ARE. IF YOU KNOW WHO YOU ARE, YOU DON'T ALLOW THE LIGHT TO DRIVE YOU. IT CAN INFORM, IT CAN ILLUMINATE, BUT YOU ARE THE MASTER OF THAT LIGHT. AND IF YOU'RE NOT THE MASTER OF THAT LIGHT, TRUST ME, SOME OTHER ENTITY WILL BE.

*YOUR JOB AS A MYSTIC IS TO SEE DEEPER THAN THE AVERAGE JOE.*

THE DARKNESS
SERVES THE LIGHT,
IF YOU ARE
CONSCIOUS.

THE DARKNESS IS
JUST THE DARKNESS,
IF YOU ARE
UNCONSCIOUS.

*I  bow my head into the light*

*where at last with simple hat I rest.*


*The flowers plucked from wilderness*

*have indeed sent me to bed.*


*And here with you my beloved*

*who shines your brilliance*


*I am still at last.*


*For so long it has been since*

*I heard your command,*

*my mind filled with chatter,*


*Now, peace, my Master.*

YOUR SOUL IS PURE — NOTHING CAN TOUCH IT. NOTHING CAN HARM IT. EVEN IF YOUR SOUL IS, AS THEY SAY, TAKEN BY THE DEVIL, EVEN IF YOU FALL IN A CHASM OF DARKNESS, YOUR SOUL REMAINS PURE. IT'S REDEEMABLE. THE SOUL OF THE EVILEST PERSON IS REDEEMABLE BECAUSE THE SOUL WAS MADE BY GOD. AND THAT IS WHAT JESUS MEANT WHEN HE SAID, "LOVE YOUR ENEMY." IT IS THAT YOU ARE TO LOVE THE PURE LIGHT WITHIN THE SOUL OF YOUR ENEMY. NOWHERE DOES IT SAY TO LOVE THE ACTIONS OF BAD BEHAVIOR.

# ALL OF OUR SOULS WANT CONNECTION TO THE MYSTERY

The path is to open up to the fact that you are a mystical being. It is time to lift the taboo of, "Oh it's 'Woo-Woo.' "

We know how "Woo-Woo" got its name, but we can't afford to make it taboo anymore, we're older and wiser now. We've had 350 years of science, so let's use it. For without scientific knowledge, the mystery becomes superstition, and superstition really is "Woo-Woo."

The day is coming where science will accept the reality of our mystical experience.

*Being a* modern-day mystic *means bringing the* divine into every mundane moment—washing the dishes, cleaning the clothes, paying the bills.

*Focus on bringing* the Light into the mundane *and you will learn how to be a great* Master of Energy.

What is real in this world? *What is real is that there are energy fields of misunderstanding and fear that are constant.* You feel them energetically. *When you are not conscious, you interpret them through the lens of your own fear story.* The world's many opposing forces *are always hitting each other.*

*Fortunately, there is a constant that you can attach yourself to, a Throne of Light, that will lift you up so that when the opposing forces do hit,* you just float right through.

The extraordinary pull of the darkness is always upon us—it takes great resistance not to be pulled into the force of darkness. But, even if you have been pulled into that world, however it looks for you, one moment of Light, one breath of truth can sustain you. That is how powerful the Light is. Nothing is more powerful than the experience of Light. Be aware of those moments of Light and like a string of pearls, the moments of Light will see you through.

*Let's find each other in the dark*
  *where your touch and the scent*
*of your breath become my dark vapor –*

*Let's find each other in the dark*
  *where the shores of our existence*
*in the swell of a shimmering magnolia*
  *become the languid woolen fields of love –*

*Let's find each other in the dark*
  *in the last utterance*
*of a violin's string plucked*
  *the river's ravine across your far wide hand –*

*Let's find each other in the dark*
  *my love, where silence melts in*
*the quiet of our forgiving.*

IF YOU DON'T HAVE A PRACTICE, WHEN YOU GO THROUGH
THE MYSTICAL GATE, WHAT DO YOU THINK HAPPENS?

YOU BECOME EXTRAORDINARILY VULNERABLE TO A WHOLE SET
OF ENERGIES THAT YOU HAVE NO IDEA WHAT YOU'RE DEALING WITH.
EVEN THOUGH THOSE ENERGIES ARE THE FOREST
YOU HAVE TO GO THROUGH TO MERGE WITH GOD, AND
GOD WANTS MORE THAN ANYTHING TO MERGE WITH YOU—

WHAT DO YOU THINK GOD DOES?

YOU'RE LITTLE RED RIDING HOOD,
YOU'RE GOING THROUGH THE WOODS, AND THERE'S A WOLF.
ON THE OTHER SIDE OF THE WOODS, THE LAND OF OZ.
GOD WANTS YOU IN OZ, BUT GOD SEES THE WOLF COMING AFTER YOU—
WHAT IS GOD GOING TO DO?

TURN YOU BACK AROUND. SPEED YOU OUT. SHUT THE GATE.
BECAUSE GOD'S MORE INTERESTED IN YOU BEING ALIVE AND WHOLE,
THAN EVEN BEING IN UNION WITH GOD.

NOW GO CL

**AN UP**

This is my practice. Every morning I spend fifteen minutes surveying the landscape of my close relationships—family, friends, then I continue on to business—work colleagues, school relationships. Then I ask myself, "How am I in this relationship? Am I clean?" God typically answers, "Now go clean up the mess."

If I'm not able to clean my mess up right away, or if I don't know how to clean up my mess, I say this prayer:

*"God, this situation is something I am going to have to revisit. Help me today to find clarity. Stay with me. Guide my actions. Walk beside me."*

# THE MESS

Then I take a deep breath, meditating on the blue pearl of light in the center of my brain. I release my breath with a gentle sigh, giving the Archangels a call. They are always ready to assist us. I pray out loud,

*"Help me Archangels to be a better person. Bring me your clarity, your strength, your healing, and your wisdom. Guide my every action until my actions become your actions. I open myself to your guidance. I am eternally thankful for your care."*

Well, that is the practice. Do this everyday. Try it for just thirty days. See what happens, because

# YOU WILL TRANSFORM

EVERY TIME YOU GIVE OF YOURSELF IN LOVING KINDNESS, COMPASSION, MERCY, CARING SERVICE, WHENEVER YOU RELIEVE THE SUFFERING OF ANYONE OR ANYTHING, YOU ARE BUILDING YOUR GOOD ENERGY. YOU ARE THE RIGHT ARM OF GOD. LIVING IN MERCY IS LIVING IN ENLIGHTENMENT.

EVERY TIME YOU RESTRAIN FROM BEING ANGRY, JEALOUS, ENVIOUS, OR SLANDEROUS, EVERY TIME YOU LET GO OF A RESENTMENT, YOU BUILD STRENGTH, RESILIENCE, RESOLVE, AND BECOME THE LEFT ARM OF GOD. YOU MUST BE A POWERFUL VESSEL OF RESTRAINT TO HOLD THE LIGHT OF GOD. THIS IS WHY RESTRAINT IS YOUR KEY TO ENLIGHTENMENT.

ACCEPT THIS AND YOUR LIFE WILL BECOME A WHOLE LOT EASIER.

Let's just say you really, really hurt somebody, made them miserable for a long time and, oh man, you messed up. If you can redeem that part of yourself, if you can repair, if you can make amends and heal that, even if the person doesn't forgive you, but if you do your part, you have redeemed that piece of brokenness in the mind of God and creation. And it may be that you were given that task to do. You went in and got your butt kicked—good thing.

That means on the journey it's time for you to go in another direction. And if you go in another direction, and you can redeem, clean up your past, make repair, heal, you will lift up a piece of that breakage. You have redeemed it. You have turned it into Light. **Darkness Serving Light.** Because in any place of darkness you can make lemonade out of lemons. That is redemption, and through redemption you receive salvation.

What do you do when negativity comes in the room? How do you handle negative energy? This is an important question to contemplate. How you handle negative energy will determine your ability to hold God's Light.

**Act In Grace. Be Noble. Show Dignity.**

Light is Pure Energy. When you have negative thoughts and actions your positive energy leaks out of your energy field into the unseen world of confusion.

**Put the plug in. Don't be a leaky puddle.**

You are giving away your life force to the beast of suffering, famine, disease and death. Every living thing is filled with light because every living thing is a creation of God. The suffering, the decay, the agony we go through, is all because this dimension is intermeshed, intertwined, with the consciousness of a beast that feeds on the light to exist. Without the light the beast would not exist.

The light would exist just fine without the beast.

The beast would not exist without the light.

*All those stories of the saints, Jesus, Buddha, the stories of Job, St. Teresa of Avila,*

*Krishna and Arjuna, Padmasambhava—they all had to go to war, a war*

*they did not want to have. They all had to slay the demon, the beast.*

*Each of us has to meet that darkness, our demon. The greatest test*

*of the journey is the slaying of the demon.*

*Nobody gets out of it.*

You

become

Quan Yin riding

a dragon. The Light is

never shown to be riding a poodle.

There are no Bodhisattvas sitting on poodles.

Are there?

They're on dragons, they're on lions, they're on stallions.

# In The Honey Jars

Time passed.  Solar winds exploded.
            Cell phones were invented.

And then I Remembered,

Who is to What
    What is to Why
        Why is to That

            The reason of "I"

The journey of Soul.

            So, I broke off a piece of myself,

( the only thing to do given the situation, an entire planet careening
through space would have become a nuisance, disrupting all order
and harmony in the cosmos. )

I took the corner

        of my being

                and alongside

                        the honey bees

    I became

            a slice of falling light—

*You have got to go into your mind and dismantle your ego structure. Dismantle it. Dissect it. Be an archeologist, dig it up.* "WHY AM I ACTING LIKE THIS? WHY AM I LOOKING AT THE WORLD THAT WAY?" *Think about it.*

*You're going to find out, you're going to discover all these voices in you that talk to you all the time in your unconscious mind.* They ARE ALWAYS RUNNING. *It's a ticker tape:*

CH CH CH CH CH...

*And when you really take the time and you look in and you start to dismantle your ego mind, you're going to be in shock at what you'll find.*

THE EGO'S LIKE, *"Whoa, wait a minute.*
*You mean that yokel down there at the*
*grocery store did a miracle? No.*
*I have to go to Tibet if I want to see a miracle."*

all assault is because the EGO misperceives

The ego thinks, "That's the only way I can be safe," and so a pattern is formed of degeneration, assault, response and assault—and as that pattern continues, the soul, that which creates miracles, hitches a ride to the stars and waits until it's safe to come back home.

For ninety percent of the people, when shame and remorse come up, the ego mechanism is so locked and loaded that, unconsciously, people batten up the hatches—build this giant monster.

You know those action-hero movies? It's a little person inside a big machine walking around killing aliens by the thousands. The little person who is manning it could, of course, never do that. Well that's what we do. We create this machine to protect how fragile we feel. Really fragile. But when you get in one of those machines, it's suddenly, "Hey, bring it on." Right? That's the ego, that's what we do. "Come on," all puffed up. "Want to fight? Come on, let's fight. I want to fight."

You don't just, **Boom, you're enlightened.**

That doesn't happen. It's a series and they

build, because the one, the big kahuna, if it

comes too early, you're toast. **You're toast.**

You're in the psychiatric ward or you leave your

body. Time to go. "Ooh, I'm in the Light."

**Yeah, but you lost your body.**


So you go to the Lords of Karma,

**"Oh, I went into the Light."** And they're like,

"Yeah, well, you big dummy, you dropped

your body while you were doing it. That

wasn't the plan. You're supposed to keep

your body. So back down to earth you go.

Next time, when you go into the Light,

**don't leave your body."**

The Angels and the Beings of Light's view of the sexual experience is completely different from our view. It's completely different from what you think. It's a whole

**SEXUALITY IS ALL EGO AND IT RARELY TOUCHES GOD**

different ball game. Human consciousness is in the ego. Right now, sexuality is all ego and it rarely touches God, but it was meant to touch God. Sex is all run by the ego. So it's complicated. But the true sexual act is holy. It was created so that we could merge with God.

Your template was set to experience and know intimacy. Intimacy happens like this: One to One. And when you know intimacy fully, that experience of truth, nurturing care, tenderness, and vulnerability is a wisdom that radiates into the world.

**RADIANCE IS INTIMACY WITH ALL THINGS**

*Beauty sits waiting*

*upon the lip*

*of a snowflake*


*while wind's*

*heart is set upon*

*his desire*


*the morning sighs*

*wake-up!*

*voluptuous reunion*

*We are One.*

Where is your beloved?
How do you know when your beloved is near?
Your soul is always longing to merge in the union of presence,
this is your soul's desire.
One of the greatest gifts you can give your soul
is the gift of divine romance, rapture.


However, sometimes
the greatest loves of our life do not last.
Love was so phenomenal.

Many times, but not always,
the greatest loves
do not last on this earth,
because the light that love creates is ...

just too bright

If you are in a practice of being hard to love, eventually people will move away. Not because they want to, but their need is love too, and it's hard to be around somebody who is, you know,

**Mr. Grumpy Pants all the time.**

Service is when you give knowing that you will not receive anything back. **That's service.** Anything else is not service. **It's a job.** If you are loving another wanting to get love back, you are not loving. You have a job and you've decided "my job is to love." Of course, it's probably the best job you'll ever have.

You are the connector
which unifies and brings
wholeness to that which
is separate. Separation is
the duality that heaven
and earth are separate,
but truth, which is love,
knows that they are one.

Your heart is your
greatest angel. Your
heart is the seed of love.

Whenever you gather
people together, whenever
you share and give loving
kindness, you are healing
our world of separation.

Right now, see in your heart a brilliant shining star. Close your eyes for a moment.

Look into this star in your heart and know you are love, and whatever is happening in your world right now, here in this brilliant star, within your heart, is peace.

In order to enter into freedom you must have a balance.
It's not enough to have a mystical experience. It's
not enough to just meditate, it's not. I wish it was.
Meditation doesn't do anything for character. Character,
the backbone, your spine, is your essence. Yet, you
can have this strong character and be completely cut
off from the fruit of the mystical. And so you suffer
because you can't taste the sweetness, because you do
have the fruit, but you cannot taste its sweetness.

have a balance

# In The Honey Jars

The mother picked up the last honey jar with only an inch left in,
    She turned the honey jar over filling her measuring cup half full.

She looked up from the kitchen table over to where her young son
    was standing in front of the fireplace.
"This is the end of the honey for this winter," she said.

The boy was playing with a fire poker,
    turning the golden embers of the fire over and over.

He hardly noticed his mother, as he was consumed by the dancing
    flames. His mother went on, "Sweet honey from the rock,
don't you worry, we'll make it through by Grace."

But her son had taken the fire poker and had run outside.
    He slashed the frozen ground, tore up the snow with his
poker, an arc—a wing, etched into the ice—mist rose.

A crackling sigh, "No, no, no more hunger." The boy's
    stomach knotted up. While overhead, an asteroid made its descent.

The boy, on seeing the flash in the sky, yelled out to his mother,
    "Mama, Mama come quick, a shooting star. It's a sign.
Soon there will be honey in the honey jars."

As you awaken, the ego begins to be washed in a river of higher consciousness, or sometimes refined in a sacred fire of higher consciousness. Once this occurs, you begin to live more of your life in your soul's consciousness than your ego's consciousness. It is here, in your soul consciousness, where you will see, feel, and experience a world that before you did not have access to. You were denied this simply because you did not know how to access it or you did not have the key to enter into the multi-dimensional realities of life, the spiritual experience of your soul. Now you do.

That's why the saints have a halo, because all around them the apertures of light are open and shining, so they glow.

*You can glow too.*

All the Beings of Light say, *"If we can get enough men and women on the ground to hold the light, we're not even talking about enlightenment because it is so misunderstood, has so much baggage… let's just forget about that… if we can just get enough people holding the light of love, love, love, not perfection, just the practice of love, if we can get enough people doing this, then when the rocket ship, Planet Earth, begins to take off, when she shakes, she will only lose a few pieces of herself and she will make it through the age of the chrysalis. She will survive. She will become her new frequency. The human soul will make it."*

We will make it. The oceans will come back. The two lions that are left will multiply. We'll get them back. We'll get the streams back. The forests will grow again and they too will come back.

We have a responsibility to set a template, to give a blessing to the next generation of kids that are coming into the world. They are the real soldiers. They are the ones that are meeting the front lines of what the ego has built—the cities, the concrete, the buildings where there is no grass or a place to plant a garden.

We have a duty, for they are our hope.

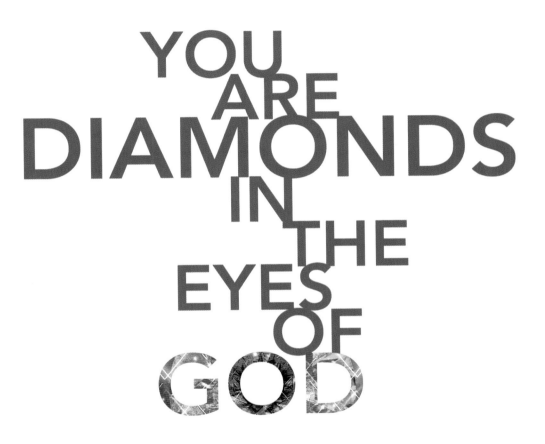

YOU ARE DIAMONDS IN THE EYES OF GOD

The actual experience of time is *changing.* Time today is not what it was twenty years ago, fifty years ago, or two hundred years ago. *It's not the same,* but because we are all here in the same dimension of time, nobody is aware that time has changed. *Because we're all in it together. Time is speeding up.*

In *2222*, there will be a great *Ascension of Mother Earth.*

At this time, the frequency of the third dimension will cease to exist—

the third dimension going into the *fourth dimension,* and this

reality will become what it was intended to be. So there will not be

death as we know it. Death will not be seen as death. It will just be a

*passage* you can take or not take because you can see what's on the

other side. *The doorways will open.*

# THERE REALLY IS ANOTHER WORLD A SISTER WORLD

# IT REALLY DOES EXIST

This world wants to be here, but she cannot, because what have we done? We have turned our back, locked the door. We have walked away. Most people lost the keys to that door, but you, as a mystic, did not lose your keys. You have them in your pocket. You just need to go a little deeper to retrieve them.

You are the ones to open the door, the gates, so that the Angels of Light can enter our world physically. Soon you will begin to feel them and see them.

Magic starts happening. Miracles start to happen. People go, "Whoa!" provided you have the keys. And what do you think comes with that, with those powerful keys?

# RESPONSIBILITY

It is time for you to step out
from being a seeker

**Magical Grace**, this splendor of creation,

is an angelic presence of your soul.


**Magical Grace** has been forgotten, but

she is all that sparkles and glitters

within you. She is that which emanates

from the mystery, her veils flying

behind her in the wind.


**Magical Grace** is open to the future, and

from her face, her heart, her hands, third

eye and navel, the dancing gems of creation

we call magic are given into our world.


and step into a template
of self-mastery.

This morning, as I opened my eyes, I felt my spirit, my soul, come back into my body in a strange new way. My spirit spoke to me, "I'm so happy to be in a body!" I said, "Really?" My spirit had never said this before. My spirit always said, "I'm out of here!" So I said, "Really?" My spirit, answering again, "Wow, yes, I'm really happy to be in a body!" Then my spirit moved my right arm. My spirit moved my left arm. My spirit started rolling around in the covers. It flexed one foot, pointed the other, rolled around again, kept saying, "I'm so happy to be in a body!" I wasn't doing any of this movement. Something else was moving my body, but that something else was me?

Then I saw my spirit as the chariot carrying my soul, the light of my soul living deep in my abdomen, like a golden egg. This is how I came to know real happiness, true joy and peace.

So I said, "Well spirit, what do we do now?" My spirit said, "I want to get up and walk around, let's start by doing that." So I got up and walked around. I went outside. I fed the birds. I fed the fish. I fed my dog. I puttered here. I puttered there.

The whole time I was aware that this spirit was in my body and that I was completely present in the Now, fully here in a state of integration with the filaments of frequency, invisible light, of our world. I was aware that I had this container for my third-dimensional reality—my body, and with this came an overwhelming love of my body. I shouted, "Body, I love you. Forgive me for judging you, blaming you, seeing you as an enemy, complaining about your aches and pains. Body, thank you for being here because without you my spirit and my soul could not be here and I could not experience this happiness." With that, I felt my consciousness transform into a state of clarity. I saw the light of Archangel Uriel. I felt the healing of Archangel Raphael, the safety of Archangel Michael, the devotion of Archangel Gabriel.

*In moments like this, the psychology of "Who am I?" becomes coherent enough that the greater mandala of our Self can in fact exist and experience the gifts, the glory, the beauty, and the joy of being in this reality.*

*We must always remember this as we sojourn through the encyclopedia of every experience we have in the world.*

ULTIMATELY, THE TRUE
MARRIAGE IS BETWEEN
YOU, THE HUMAN BEING,
AND GOD. AND WHEN
YOU ARE IN A MARRIAGE
WITH THE CREATOR,
YOU ARE IN A MARRIAGE
WITH EVERY CELL, EVERY
MOLECULE, OF ALL THAT IS.

AND THAT IS HOW
YOU ENTER INTO THE
KINGDOM WITHIN AND
THAT FREQUENCY IS
WHERE WE ARE GOING.

# In The Honey Jars

Falling through a crescent
      torn from atmosphere,

the bees and I descended—

flying into time, hitting the fabric wall,
     ripping from the wilderness

wings burned Icarus
     first to moon, then to earth—

I landed on the mountain snow
     screaming to the wind,
          "I have arrived!"

The wind came howling back,
     the boy ran, the bees cried—
mother chasing after son,

"Miracle of Gabrielle! An angel has come!"

The boy lurched into the fire of the bees

     extinguishing himself into the prophecy.

# In The Honey Jars

Honey melted from the poker
    formed a pool on the ground.

        A golden urn of redemption that sat alone.

          Mother and Son

the witness—as Isaiah touched the night—speaking,

    "Be Still and know that I Am Here Now."

And the formation of what was to be known
    as the miracle of winter's birthing,
the boy and his mother went inside their home.

For they found there on the window shelf
    eight full jars of honey with one more in the center.

On the days to come passers-by would comment on
    the nine lights of winter that became
        the hope of the prophets of the coming age.

ONE
POUND
PURE
HONEY

The End

## We wish to thank

**Jennifer Chisik** for always helping in a million ways.

**Ananda Grimm** and **Akasha Lee** for their tireless work in transcribing the volumes and volumes of Deirdre's talks.

Deirdre's daughter **Leilah Franklin** for stepping in at critical moments and keeping us on course.

For appearing in these pages: Endre's daughters **Eva, Katalin** and **Csilla Balogh,** Deirdre's son **Eric Franklin, Amely Greeven** and her daughter **Patience Williams.**

**Shina Sebring** for reminding us of the wealth of knowledge patiently waiting in the transcripts.

**Dana Schwartz** for putting a bug in William's ear about the need for a book of quotes.

**Jill Hawkins,** graphic designer extraordinaire, for the layout of this book. To see more, visit: jillhawkinsdesign.com

**Bill** and **Gayle Gladstone** of Waterside Productions for believing in the book when it was barely half-done and then publishing the finished work.

And of course, those beings "on the other side" for guidance, inspiration, and relentlessly pushing us to do something.

**For more surprises, mystical wisdom and insight, join us at: BookOfSurprises.com**

Copyright 2016 Captured Light Industries
CapturedLight.biz

Published by Waterside Press
waterside.com

ISBN 978-1-943625-93-2     First Edition

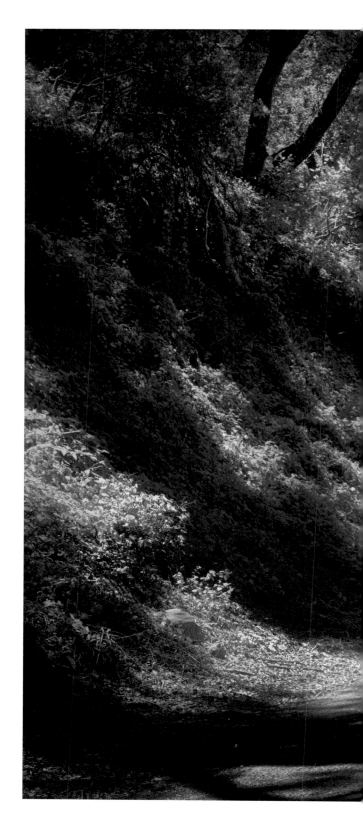

Since her early years in Memphis, Tennessee, **Deirdre Hade** has been an artist and a visionary, writing poetry and conversing with the mystical worlds. As a ballet dancer and choreographer recognized by Robert Joffery, she performed throughout the country and founded the dance ensemble, "Celebrations to the Sacred." At sixteen, her mother diagnosed with terminal breast cancer, Deirdre discovered the healing power of light, enabling her mother to live thirteen years longer than expected. As the founder of Radiance Healing and Meditation, Deirdre has guided people worldwide, teaching them to harness their own inner wisdom and healing potential. She is currently writing her story of life as a modern day mystic. To learn more, visit: DeirdreHade.com.

**William Arntz** started his professional career as a research laser physicist, working on "Star Wars" high energy lasers. He then moved on to software, writing "AutoSys"—an automated job control system currently in use by most Fortune 500 companies. He sold that company, retired, but then decided to make a film: creating, producing and directing *What the BLEEP Do We Know!?*, an exploration of spirituality, quantum physics, neurology and outrageous possibilities. The film and the companion book, with editions in over twenty languages, were international hits. He is once again talking about retirement, although that is doubtful as he is married to one Deirdre Hade (see above). For more info: CapturedLight.biz.

**Endre Balogh** is an internationally known concert violinist, having performed as a soloist with orchestras such as the Berlin Philharmonic and eminent musicians Zubin Mehta, Vladimir Horowitz and André Watts. He is also a sought-after photographic artist. The Professional Photographers of California named him "Number Two" among the "Top Ten Photographers" and he is one of only thirty five photographers worldwide to achieve "Diamond" status in the 2015 Professional Photographers of America International Competition. To see more, visit: EndresArt.com.